Journey to Wisdom

Bipolar Reflections

Cynthia Weston

Devlyn Press
Jericho, Vermont
2013

Printed in the United States of America by
Devlyn Press
P.O. Box 41
Jericho, VT 05465

Available from bookstores and online.
Signed copies are available direct from the publisher:
email: devlynpress@comcast.net

ISBN: 978-061573778-2

To John,
The gentle and quiet man
Who gave me courage and strength
When I had none,
Always walking next to me on my journey
To healing, wisdom, and compassion.

Contents

Introduction xv

Acknowledgments xvii

Part One
Reflections

I Am 21

Awakening 22

Melancholia 23

Transcience 24

Now 25

Futility 26

Passages 27

Echoes 28

Gifts 29

Resonance 30

Depression 31

Unsolved 32

Part Two
Difficult Reality

Psyche 35

Eternity 36

Identity Crisis 37

Silence 38

The "I" Who Is " Me" 39

Duplicity 40

Rubble 41

Chaos 42

Unchained Despair 43

War 44

Beginnings 45

Sealed Closure 46

Never Knowing 47

Winter Spirits 48

Paces 49

Difficult Reality 50

Reclamation 51

Hell 52

Dirge 53

Defeated … Again 54

Imperfection 55

Insanity 56

Underdog 57

Panther 58

The Night Has Been Cast 59

Deliverance 60

Madness 61

A Last Goodbye 62

Suffering is Optional 63

Searching 64

Haze 65

Circles 66

Lost 67

Time 68

Vulnerability 69

Part Three
Looking Ahead

Dawn 73

Scorn 74

Reaching 75

SP3R323 76

Duality 77

Only the Alone 78

Empowerment 79

Sand Castles 80

Life Cycle 81

Turning Back the Pages 82

The Middle 84

Giving 85

Travels 86

Dichotomy 87

Friendship 88

Where I Am 89

Just Once 90

Part Four
Beauty

Master of Arts 93

Joy to the World 94

Glorious Beauty 95

Wealth 96

Peace 97

Haiku 98

Where You Are 101

Thunder Hole 102

Just for Today 103

Renewal 104

Country 'scape 105

Part Five
Wisdom

Reality 109

Enlightenment 110

Sentience 111

Worldly Goods 112

Suspended Judgment 113

A Different Future 114

Doves of Peace

Let Her Be 116

Let Me Be 118

Let Us Be 120

About the Author 123

Journey to Wisdom

Bipolar Reflections

Introduction

Poetry is an art form that reveals beauty, compassion, pain, and wisdom, and it has guided me to understand the truth of a Higher Power. As a poet, I found the wisdom and power to act with a measure of acceptance and grace as I experienced events that changed my life.

Poetry is only one way to share the journey of Bipolar Disorder. Each poem on the following pages is my spirit written on paper. When mental, emotional, and physical strength fade, I open my treasure box and grasp strategies learned throughout my journey. I believe we can all have our own treasure box, with one of the strategies being writing.

Poetry surrounds me without my even thinking about it—a congratulations card for the blessing of a new child, a Bible verse for a family grieving at a funeral, words from a favorite song. In reading and writing poetry, I realize others feel all the same emotions that I feel. The knowledge that I am not alone in how I feel, but that I share in humanity's feelings, gives me the strength and courage to meet the adversities of life.

Poetry is universal, found everywhere and in each of us. I enjoy capturing that essence of humanity I experience in my unique way. To maintain progress and stability, managing Bipolar Disorder is a full-time job. It is my hope that others with Bipolar Disorder can continue to fight their own demons through writing poetry or other expressive genres. Writing during a depressive or manic episode can create a calm and soothing rhythm.

The writing of poetry is one of the gifts that helped me to reach the inner peace I had been searching for most of my life. My inner peace is now a part of the essence of who I am. Writing is only one therapeutic strategy I have used on my long journey to peace and contentment. Discover your own voice to soften the despair of depression or the dangers of mania. You, too, may find that writing is "a way through it."

Acknowledgments

My deep gratitude goes to Pat Goudey O'Brien, my copy and design editor, who worked tirelessly in her efforts. Her help in structuring and re-structuring this book was above the call of duty. Her encouragement and support to make this endeavor the best book possible deserve my tremendous thanks. It was Pat who made my book a reality.

Deep thanks go to Dr. John Edwards, who was relentless in his efforts to convince me to publish my poetry. Without his honest and convincing words over many years, I would not have finally found the right time.

I am especially grateful to the members of my writing group for accepting me into their circle and accepting me for the person I am. Their quiet and gentle editing suggestions were always thoughtful and professional and have allowed me to grow at my own pace. I admire and respect all of them and am proud to be a part of a writing group with authors who have exceptional talent. Thank you Grant Corson, Richard Mindell, Joe Nelson, Marie Flaim Tedford, and Ted Tedford.

And thank you to my best friend, Linda Charkin, who encouraged me to publish the poetry of my bipolar journey.

Reflections

I AM

I am.
I am.
I am not bad.

I am.
I am.
I am melancholic and discordant.

I am.
I am.
I am fractured and damaged.

I am.
I am.
I am wanting to be.

I am.
I am.
I want you to see what's inside of me.

I am.
I am.
I am unity.

I am.
I am.
You see. I have the "I" who is "me."

I am.
I am.
I am free.

Awakening: Path of Memories

I need to be reminded of nature's splendor of a thousand years:

The royal blossoms
The snowflakes fluttering
The pair of white doves
Clear water cascading

I will remember:

The lightness of the human spirit
Human dignity

I will relinquish my soul as a whole:

Building life on a shaky foundation
The empty spaces
The shadows of death
Being saddled with the Darkness

I will banish:

The two-edged sword
Self-torment

Melancholia:

A

state of being

null and void.

Transcience

Happiness
is
a rare bright light
that flickers
and quickly dies.

Now

Heaven and Hell
What a terribly restricted view of death.

Futility

arises

upon

the death

of hope.

Passages

Life is

a passing moment

in a journey

with no destination.

Echoes

Resignation

resounds

within the deadened cavity

of the mind.

Gifts

To forgive is to set the

prisoner free

and then discover

you were the prisoner.

Resonance

Aloneness
and
silence
echo
against
the
disintegrated
walls
of
a
crumbled
mind.

Depression

A raven blackness

filling the silent space

of its own vacuum.

Unsolved

Depression is not death on the inside.

It is the search for truth on the outside.

Difficult Reality

Psyche

I'm Nobody
living in the land
of Nothingness.

One day,
I was Somebody.

Eternity

Lost spirit-soul wanders the earth,
Drifting aimlessly,
Searching for unencumbered solitude,
Peace and solace forever elusive.

Identity Crisis

I hear the silence of the pain
as the Darkness tiptoes back.

I see the words of despair
as the lips of the Shroud do not speak.

I touch the scent of your False Hope
in breaking a life cycle.

I sense my insidious return.
I am the words of Failure.

Yes, You pervade the senses of my life
as confusion reigns and conquers.

Silence

Silent sobs,
Swelling my soul,
Waiting to weep,
As my Self listens.

Alone in silence,
Life moves on graciously.
Others see its brightness
And hear its laughter.

Life's pace slows leisurely
As the soul releases the sobs
So gently, so silently,
As the world passes by in all its regalia.

The "I" Who is "Me"

Lost Soul
wandering in the haze
looking for the "I"
who is "Me."

Silently I cry,
biding my time, waiting to be heard
by loved ones to ask,
"What happened to You?
Where did You go?"

"Where did you lose You?
Did someone take You away?"
I scream with no words, no sounds,
hoping they will see the unseen,
listen to the unheard.

From the empty, robbed soul
will come their understanding.
The Blackness carries me
down the dark vortex.
My soul cannot escape.

Duplicity

Please, Mr. Doc Man.
Fix me a cocktail.
Make it strong.
Lots of Klonopin.
More of Percocet.
Handsful of Xanax.
Bottles of Valium.
Don't forget the Fiorinal.

No ice, please.
I'll be cold soon enough.
Thanks, Mr. Doc Man.

Rubble

Four closing walls,
Collapsing floors,
Falling ceilings,
Crumbled shatters remain.

Death is imminent.
Come quickly,
Silent one.

Chaos

Discouraging.
Difficult.

To feel that life is
more than good,

Only to find
it's as dark as ever.

Unchained Despair

Unspoken dreams
gone silent.

Yesterday's security
fallen to ashes.

Today's fears
overwhelming.

Future days
all undone.

Running scared,
nowhere to go.

No place to rest.
Run, run, run
as fast as I can.

Chase the demons away.
Leave the fears behind.

Run, Run, Run.

War

The children pecked at me,
leaving me bloodied
from the daily battles.
Little did they know
they emptied my soul.

Daughter and husband
let me integrate their woes
into my lost and empty being.

Let time pass over me,
not alarm me.
A sense of urgency
below this façade,
weeping the unseen tears
they will never know.

A day, a week, a month,
time on end
flow with me
to find the fragmented spirit
to rebuild and reclaim
the "I" who is "Me."

Let me endorse "I"
who is not the Blackness.
Give me a timely break
from a fragile cocoon,
slowly creating the"I"
who is "Me."

Beginnings

Marble statue, strong and shiny,
heartened being, a tale to tell.
Woeful soul, a deep dark hole,
plaintive eyes, mind decomposed.

Marble statue, dressed in armor,
not a chink visible.
Facelessness built on sand,
life trembling in the balance.

Words unspoken,
Tears unseen.
Essence surrendered,
mind insubstantial.

A fissure creates fear.
A tear may be shed.
Control is loosened.
Empty spaces surround.

He has passed.
I cannot say goodbye.
No longer have I a stronghold.
A love is lost.

Sealed Closure

Silently sitting,
Eyes not a drop.
Loneliness hidden.
Dignity visible.

Shadow of the death,
Stronghold armored.
Integrity a sanctuary.
Pain now concealed.

Need to say goodbye.
Alone.
Aloneness they must give me.
Grief denied.

"We must leave now.
Mom has to leave."

Not a pebble allowed me.
No last sound.
No closure for me.

Never Knowing

It's hard for you to know
how one day I feel so euphoric
and sure I can do anything,
even if it might be impossible.

How can you understand the next day
when I feel deeper than the Mariana Trench?
Just a thin piece of string
from ending it all.

Winter Spirit

The outside is frigid and dark.
My soul is barely tepid.
My spirit is cool to the world.
My being is cold to humanity.

Paces

Enervation emanates from
a ravaged soul.
Self-emptiness merges a companion
with aloneness.
Apathy, a constant foe,
leadens the emptiness with despondence.
Inside the mind's darkened room
the soul's death knell tolls on Death Row.
The long walk has commenced,
woeful melancholia shuffling laboriously.

Difficult Reality

What does life matter?
Life isn't living.
Living just feels like dying.

Reclamation

Death of Innocence,
Purity tainted.
Half-shadows held in abeyance.
The Ghost hovers inside the Haunter.

Writhing in pain,
Withering soul,
Secludes the mind
And confines the Spirit.

For the passenger
The Darkness engulfs the Child.
Silent sobs prevail uninvited and unwanted
Adrift in a world of her own.

In this world,
But not of it.

Hell

Retribution for the evil ones.
Fiery inferno fueled by earthly spirits.
Eternal fury, no confessionals.

Negotiation time has passed.
No divine intervention here.
Did He ever listen anyway?

Dirge

In the wasteland of life
hopes and dreams are irreclaimable.
Desolation of the mind's landscape
reflects the muted browns, grays and blacks
of the adversities of life.

Defeated ... Again

Troubled and stormy,
bowed in the face of defeat,
humbled again.

I am the prey pursued
by the Black Death.
Talons of victory stretching
to tear out my soul.

Imperfection

Reclusive and morose,
spiral dancing
down the Black Hole.
Emotional bludgeoning,
lack of psychic endurance
interlace
the universe of ambiguity.

Insanity

I cannot separate myself from the
Darkness that engulfs me.
I cannot detach from the
craziness as it touches me.
The ebb and flow of their insidiousness
conquer the cancerous mind.

I am beset once again with
the loss of human dignity.

Underdog

You tiptoed in so silently,
like the padded paws of the lynx,
the stalking feline.
You readied your body for its
deadening destruction.

Ah, but first you had
to play your game of
cat and mouse.
That's the fun.

When will the stalking end?
The mouse is losing again.
Your keen-sightedness triumphed again.
The underdog never wins.

Panther

A worthy opponent, indeed.
Blackness shrouded, my enemy,
lurking within my soul,
quiet as the falling snow,
ready to conquer its prey.

The Night Has Been Cast

Melancholy gray descending
into dark, dank joylessness,
gloom crowding in on me,
a sense of despair and emotional nakedness,
a habit of recurrence.

Mind continues its unsettling despondency,
ensnared in a suffocating realistic hopelessness,
in the black-out of the weather of depression,
fear of the inward death,
the right path is lost in the vast, dark woods.

Deliverance

Death sent me an invitation.
Should I RSVP?

Madness

Each passing blight
leaves the mind fallow
and marked by scars.

Darkened mind,
disordered reason,
reign supreme within.

The disharmony of the mind and brain.

A Last Goodbye

Shadows of the dead.

Only the surviving souls of life's Darkness understand.

The others remain selfish.

Suffering is Optional

Neck hanging from rope.
Silent sleeping in a closed car.
Streaming blood from the wrists.
Destroyed face among the craggy rocks.

Disbelief is mine.
Family and friends ask, "Why?"
Suicide is the last dedication to one's pain.
Only those who know the Darkness can answer "why."

Her family surrounds me.
They hold me in their arms.
Their grief is on the outside.
Peace at any price, I sigh.

Searching

What is depression

if not a journey

of self-hatred and self-love?

Haze

Dismal somberness
at dawn,
wakened to the mind's vaporish fog,
hangs from today's clouds.

The darkened meandering of paths leads to the end.
Where to turn?

Circles

Stripped of defenses against the Darkness,
the blots and smears remind of life's losses.
A brewing storm is in a mind rotting
to prepare its assault on me.

Human dignity stands powerless
against the madness of mania.
Insanity wreaks its malice
in life's nightmare.

The two-edged sword becomes
one entwined enemy.

No boulevard of life becomes a sanctuary.
The circular mirror reflects the
continual chaos of the mind.
I can never say goodbye again.

I can only accept the
mangled mind of craziness.
My soul is a deep hole,
And a madness sublime.

Lost

Who am I?
I lost myself when I wasn't looking.
Does that mean my Self is dead?
It feels like it.

Time

Yesterday I was.

Today I am.

Tomorrow I may be.

Vulnerability

I hear the Silence of the Pain
as the Darkness tiptoes back.
I see the words of despair
as the lips of the Shroud do not speak.
I touch the scent of your false love
in breaking a life cycle.
I sense your arrival
insidiously recurring.

Yes, You pervade the senses of my life,
but my strength still reigns and conquers.
I am the words of success.

Looking Ahead

Dawn

Naked in the wind I stand,
Arms outstretched, eyes pleading
Toward the heavens,
Alone, unprotected, vulnerable
To life's fated tribulations,
Pleading to whom, I no longer know.

Not to God so cruel – NO!
But to myself, all that I have,
Even then, I'm not so sure.
I lost myself to cancer of the mind.

Trembling and standing eastward,
I listen to myself,
Ready to give thanks
To the dawning of a new day.

Scorn

Devilish Demon,
you arrived
to kick my feet
from under me.

I won't stay down long.
My strength will help me rise.
My mind will grapple with yours.
I'll leave my lethargic retreat.

My fear will disappear.
I will rise again.

Reaching

Anchored in the past,
exiled in the mind,
waiting for the escape to come,
for only I can reach me.
Only my weeping
transcends the limitations of the mind.

SP3R323

No friend have I seen,
although I know they are there
waiting for my call
to help me with my needs.

No family have I seen,
no family knows I'm here.
A daughter who doesn't care
anywhere that I am.

My dark-dressed Foe I have seen
running hard to build himself in me.
Little does the Darkness know
that I will take the show.

So little does the Darkness know
that the "I" who is "Me"
will arrive with the sun
and the crisp, clear air.

Duality

Quelled by its codes of silence,
the ebb and flow of feelings
create unity of the mind

Savor the tapestry of the mind's eye
with its echoes of yin and yang.

Only the Alone

Ponder, "aloneness" is not quite so bad.
Only one person's pain exists.
Only one person's guilt cries.
Only one person's shame hides.
Only one person's to blame.

Only the Alone.

Only the tears to shed.
Only the fears to face.
Only the silent sobs to hear.
Only He to renounce.

"Aloneness is not so bad."

Empowerment

There she stands in the shadows,
A safe haven surrounds.
She is wishing a light to break the silence.

The warrior inside is crumbling.
Her armor dented and vulnerable.
Her shield has been worn by battle.

The soul is strong.
The mind tends to the fears of guilt and blame.
The Spirit is perpetual.

She will arise from the ashes of the shadows.
Powerless she will not be.
Serrated edges no longer will slash the soul.

Sand Castles

I can detach
and not be isolated.
I can be in control
and be free.

The dying of the mind
flowers in the heart.
Take a risk. Take a chance.
Own my power.

A lightening of spirit
creates castles in the air.
The Boulevard of Life
validates its offer of human dignity.

The mirror stands before me
reflecting negative illusions.
I am no one's victim,
except my own.

Unconditional self-love sacrifices
the wrinkling of the mind.
Gentleness with myself
helps bring back my soul.

Life Cycle

Memories always live.
Life never dies.
Forgiving is in the heart.
Forgetting is in the mind.

Turning Back the Pages

Pain shrouded by love,
Memories hidden by silence,
The past a tomb of death.

Generosity echoed by compassion,
Pride shining within the depth of his eyes,
A strength not to be forgotten.

His lifelong dream fulfilled by his "little one."
His sleep of death a rainbow.
"Someday I will be part of your life again."

Turning the Pages Ahead

An abandoned bond nullified,
Splintered and fragmented,
Suffocating and disconnected.

In the detachment of the soul,
Her rejection of life
Surfaces from the arsenal of her being.

The future barren of acceptance,
The abyss grows deeper,
The cracks and fissures creating a minefield.

Today

The stream trickles over the rocks.
The high flowers wave with their splendorous colors.
The man sits waiting patiently by the stream
Echoing his love and pride.
"Come, My Dear, I've been missing you."
"Me, too, Dad," I answer.

Reality sets in with the climbing of the mountains.

The Middle

Lost was my soul.
Despair took the lead.
Desperation succumbed to the turmoil.
I brought grief, fear and loss.

Trembling was in the balance.
Trust was in the clouds.
Faith was an empty space.
Words were mute.

The Black Darkness governed my soul.
Risk was rooted in fear.
Faith needed replenishment.
Black clouds let the rain fall.

He raised the blinds to let in the sunshine.
I could watch the clouds in
The sanctuary of peace.
Surrender became my survival.

The foundation is now stronger.
The marble statue is gone.
Trust and faith are no longer held in refuge.
Tears are learning to be shed.

Giving

I gave you my heart.
I gave you my soul.
I gave you my love.
I gave you my all.
But to me, you gave back none.

Travels

Morpheus tiptoes to the Darkness
with his flickering candlelight,
whispering words of wisdom,
placing the shroud ever so gently
for the final journey of the tormented soul.

No more yesteryears of stark sorrow.
The sun slowly rises over the mountain
offering hope and happiness for the future
in this new world of mine.
Affirmation of the soul
is confirmed.

Dichotomy

Long is the night.
Black is the sky.
Thrashing is the wind.
Dead is the soul.

Bright is the day.
Yellow is the sun.
Swaying is the flower.
Alive is the soul.

Friendship

Thank you, Death,
for your kindly invitation.
I need to pass this time.
Defeatism doesn't suit me.
Deliverance is traveling in my direction.

Where I Am

Sitting quietly on the grassy lea
dotted with vibrant colors of wild flowers,
listening to the trickling brook,
as the water flows over the stones.

Gently holding my hands
with calm smiles,
I finally have the
peace and contentment
I always sought.

Just Once

Let my mind just once be in rhythmic synchrony.
Let it just once stay in a magical and mystical serenity.
Let it just once let me soar with the majesty of the eagle.
Let it just once let the mind's flower seeds
Nurture me with care, so rare.

Today, just once, I will live these golden moments.

Beauty

Master of Arts

Nature's Spring tiptoes in slowly
with its fruits of beauty.

A few sunbeams slowly melt
the piles of snow
as spring readies itself.

The bloom of tender crocuses
offers us the awakening of Spring.

Two bluebirds have their spring fly-in
charming each other,
chasing back and forth among the trees.

A robin perches on a branch
as another comes to join.

The splendor of Nature's Spring
gives us the sights of a thousand eyes,
its transcendent gift of life.

Joy to the World

Awaken as dawn spreads its glory,
Turn on the heart with wonder.
Accept the tranquility of this golden moment.
Raise the blinds to let sunbeams in.

Live in harmony with nature.
Wonder at the soft petals of a rose.
Respect the majesty covering the abundance of land.
Shower yourself with the beauty of an ordinary tree.

Harmonize with the clouds that float with ease.
Thrill at the trees standing like memorials to the sky.
Feel the crystal raindrops.
Glow with the rainbow of colors.

Own the nobility of being human and own the richness of love,
The beauty of a tender, gentle touch.
Worship the beauty of nature.
Experience the calmness it shares.

Glorious Beauty

A gentle breeze encircles and sprays me,
like the softness of love.
As I walk on the grains of sand,
the seagulls soar in an azure blue sky.
Gliding gulls alight on the rocks and ocean
As smooth as a shiny piece of marble.

I am engulfed by the warmth of the sun.
My soul awakens to view the sunbeams on the water.
My Miraculous Ocean!

Wealth

All is calm and quiet on the ocean
as it affirms the silence of the air.
Its sanctuary embraces me.
A serenity reflects my soul.

Walking along the beach with sands between my toes
allows me a bright and expansive view of beauty.
This wealth is vast and horizons far
where water merges with the sky.

Walk to the sun.
Embrace the warmth of precious gifts.
Watch the heavenly doves.
Walk the shores of the ocean.

Peace

Aloneness retreated,
Blue skies opened wide,
Sunshine warms her quintessence.

Rocked like a babe,
Caressed by the sea,
Nurtured by the crisp air.

In the present, lulled to serenity.
She cannot return home.
Her life belongs to the sea.

Haiku

meadows of flowers
grasses swaying in the field
embrace summer's view

rippling river current
offers delightful laughter
dogs swim, children splash

rainbow arches awe
an audience of life's smiles
how the world could be

light slivers of dawn
comforting birds singing now
sleepy eyes open

undressing she bares
her arm to the biting cold
winter's passion play

boughs laden with snow
tranquil crystals, lacy flakes
snowflakes cleanse the air

gentle blossoms bloom
fragrant flowers drenched with dew
myriad colors

clouds float with ease
live in nature's harmony
puffy clouds abound

castles built of sand
blue waves crash with spirit
sand erodes away

colorful tree leaves
swirling in the crisp fall air
floating to the ground

canada geese fly
in perfect "V" formation
taking turns to lead

large cumulus clouds
floating in azure blue sky
lifting the gliders

crunch of colored leaves
footprints crumble the carpet
before snow comes

Where You Are

Dear Mom,
Dear Dad,
you are finally there
together.

Sitting quietly on the grassy lea,
dotted with vibrant colors of wildflowers,
listening to the trickling brook,
as water flows over stones.

Gently holding hands
with calm smiles,
you finally have
peace and contentment.

Together.

Thunder Hole

Some days I wonder if I want
to visit the ocean.

Other days I wonder if I want
to be part of the ocean.

Just for Today

Light clouds and blue sky blending together,
Cool breeze upon her humbled face.
Her soul is no longer hidden,
Arisen from the sea.

Today she is not cold.

Rebuilt strength, life awakens,
She asks, "Why does life elude me?"
Deep Self replies, "Just because."
Answers there are not.

Today she is not cold.

Dancing are the waves,
Aloneness underground,
Voices silent, quiet within.
Oh Ocean, my Ocean!

Today I am not cold.

Renewal

Engulfed in the ethereal air
Touching my soul,
I smell the salty ocean.
I see the seagulls swoop.
I hear the lapping waves.
I touch the flowing tide.
I feel the ocean's womb.
I taste the ocean's wealth.

Country 'scape

Endless swirls of color,
Flowers flowing in the wind,
Dancing in the breeze,
Colors as bright as an arched rainbow.
Flowers stand with grace
As a wealth of precious gifts.
Untold richness
Abounds in nature's fertile fields.
Royal blossoms sparkle with joy.
Fragile flowers to behold.
An art palette not to be missed.

Wisdom

Reality

Sometimes I forget to remember:

- the insensitivity of the ignorant
- the imperfection of humanity
- the fragility of love
- the frailty of hope

Sometimes I just wish I could remember to forget.

Enlightenment

Sometimes I forget to remember:

The echoes of life
The wealth of the ocean
The radiance of life
The glow of a pregnant woman
The innocence of a child

Never may I forget:

The nobility of being human
The harmony of love and trust
The peace offering of forgiveness
The tenderness of pain
The elegant simplicity of life

Above all, let me practice:

Being humble
Being compassionate
Being dignified
Being accepting
Being forgiving

Sentience

Cultivate tolerance.
Even of the intolerant.

Listen more than you speak.
Be profoundly non-judgmental in your silence.

Respect people,
Ere they respect you.

Love the child you were.
Be gentle with the person you are.

Practice dignity as the cornerstone of life,
Reminiscent of justice and mercy.

Hear the voice of integrity.
Affirm the truth of tenderness.

Feel compassion.
Embrace another's pain.

Endure the impermanence of anguish.
Restore the pain to courage.

Accept the journey of wisdom.
Nurture the perpetual quietness of the mind.

Validate the treasures of life –
Forgiveness, integrity, respect, dignity, compassion, tolerance.

Worldly Goods

Earth.
Strength from Power.

Sky.
Compassion from Love.

Air.
Love from Breath.

Water.
Calmness of Being.

Suspended Judgment

Independence is safety.
Love is trust.
Independence is judgment.
Love is security.
Independence is powerful.
Love is tenuous.

Independence is a destination.
Love is a journey.
Independence is confidence.
Love is spontaneity.
Independence is being right.
Love is willing to be wrong.

Independence is rejection.
Love is acceptance.
Independence is a lonely place.
Love is home.
Independence is confining.
Love is opening.

A Different Future

Sometimes, the lights of my life
will dim and flicker into darkness.

Maybe, just maybe, a blazing star
will fall through my final darkness
and guide me to another universe.

There, other souls like mine,
will embrace me and bring me
into their community of love and acceptance.

More importantly, differences won't matter
because wisdom will rule.

DOVES OF PEACE

Just Let Her Be

Just let her be –
to wander her path of life
and discover the castles in the air.

Just let her be –
to look upward to the sky
and appreciate the clouds that flow with ease.

Just let her be –
to sparkle with joy
and feel delight as the dawn spreads its glory.

Just let her be –

to possess the richness of life

and respect the nobility of being human.

Just let her be –

to live in harmony with the beauty of nature

and awaken to sunbeams reflecting on the lake.

Just let her be –

to have a lightness of spirit

and live in serenity.

Just let her be –

to have a golden moment

and raise her eyes to let the sun shine in.

Just let her be –

to drift in the world she owns

and slowly walk the avenues of her life.

Just let her be –

to own a blossom of dreams

and reminisce on the richness of love.

Just Let Her Be

Just Let Me Be

Just let me be –
to exist as the person I was meant to be
without living in judgment of me.

Just let me be –
to live in my present life
without critical words and actions.

Just let me be –
to live, give and care
without invalidating my peace and contentment.

Just let me be –
to nurture myself with nature
and not distort what I value in life.

Just let me be –
to follow my right path
and not try to control and conquer me.

Just let me be –

to live with my mind's thoughts and words

and not dispose your rage and pain on me.

Just let me be –

to travel through paths of memories

and not cause pain that crushes the soul.

Just let me be –

to practice my wisdom and compassion

and not degrade me with prejudices.

Just let me be –

to live in the present

and not denigrate my integrity and dignity.

Just Let Me Be

Just Let Us Be

Just let us be –
to follow the intricate labyrinth of winding passages
and find our own paths of acceptance.

Just let us be –
to experience the fragility of humanity
and value our personal beliefs of one's frailty.

Just let us be –
to view through the stained glass window
and not know what secrets lay behind it.

Just let us be –
to remember the empty spaces where there are none
and still feel the evolution of peace.

Just let us be –
to survive the inhumanity of man to man
and face the difficulties of life in our own ways.

Just let us be –
to own our power to be the forgiver and forgiven
and accept that there is a saving grace.

Just let us be –
to feel attachment, not succumbing to fear and loss,
and end the process of letting go.

Just let us be –

to practice mindful compassion

and have the power to live with acceptance.

Just let us be –

to remember to live our words and actions

to breathe a life of dreams.

Just Let Us Be.

About the Author

Cynthia Weston is a retired Consulting Teacher/Learning Specialist. Her poetry has been published in *A Blossom of Dreams: the International Library of Poets* and *A Celebration of Poets: Showcase Edition*. She enjoys reading, writing, and the serenity and beauty of nature. She lives in Vermont.

CPSIA information can be obtained at www.ICGtesting.com
Printed in the USA
BVOW070511050313

314714BV00001B/8/P

9 780615 737782